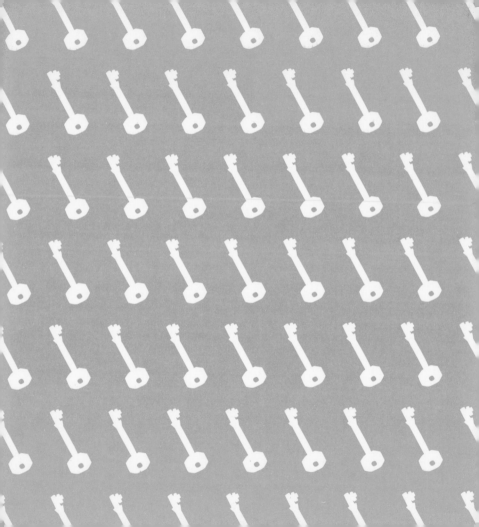

WHERE THE F*CK ARE MY KEYS?!

AN HACHETTE UK COMPANY
WWW.HACHETTE.CO.UK

SUMMERSDALE PUBLISHERS LTD
PART OF OCTOPUS PUBLISHING GROUP LIMITED
CARMELITE HOUSE
50 VICTORIA EMBANKMENT
LONDON
EC4Y 0DZ
UK

WWW.SUMMERSDALE.COM
PRINTED AND BOUND IN CHINA
ISBN: 978-1-80007-699-0

SUBSTANTIAL DISCOUNTS ON BULK QUANTITIES OF SUMMERSDALE BOOKS
ARE AVAILABLE TO CORPORATIONS, PROFESSIONAL ASSOCIATIONS AND
OTHER ORGANIZATIONS. FOR DETAILS CONTACT GENERAL ENQUIRIES:
TELEPHONE: +44 (0) 1243 771107 OR EMAIL: ENQUIRIES@SUMMERSDALE.COM.

WHERE THE F*CK ARE MY KEYS?!

HUGH JASSBURN

Find them

WE'VE ALL BEEN THERE: BUSY DAY AHEAD, RUNNING LATE, BUT NO SIGN OF YOUR LESSER-SPOTTED KEYS! JUST WHERE THE F*CK HAVE THEY GOT TO? WHAT WOULD NORMALLY INDUCE ALL KINDS OF RAGE IN REAL LIFE CAN NOW BE A SOURCE OF MENTAL STIMULATION AND AMUSEMENT WITH THE HELP OF THIS COMICAL COLLECTION OF VISUAL PUZZLES. FIND YOUR KEYS IN A RANGE OF EVERYDAY AND NOT-SO-EVERYDAY ENVIRONMENTS – AND TRY NOT TO SWEAR.

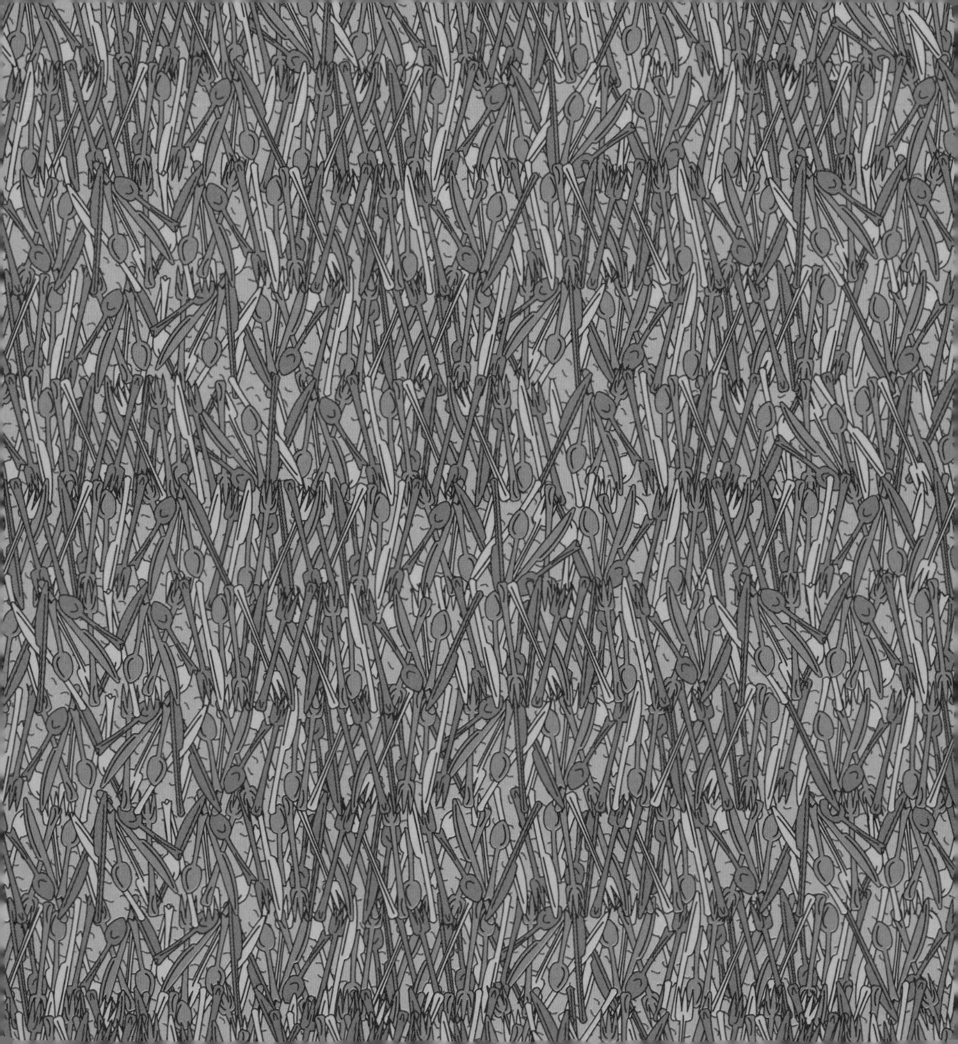

DID YOU DROP THEM IN THE SOCK PILE?

RUMMAGE AMONG THE POTTED PLANTS

ARE THEY IN YOUR TOOL BOX?

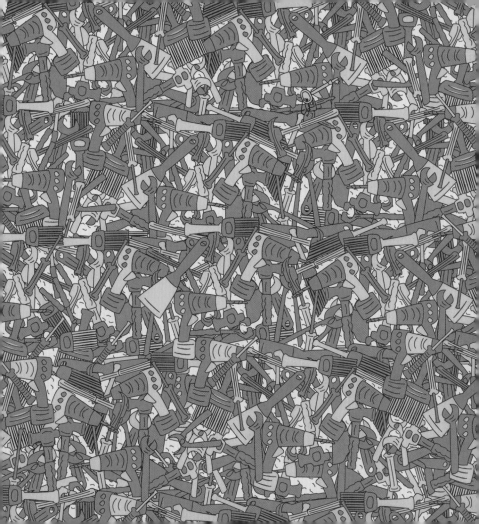

GET IN WITH THE CREEPY-CRAWLIES

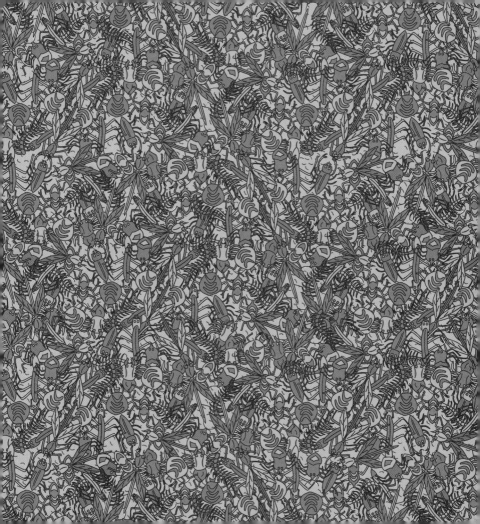

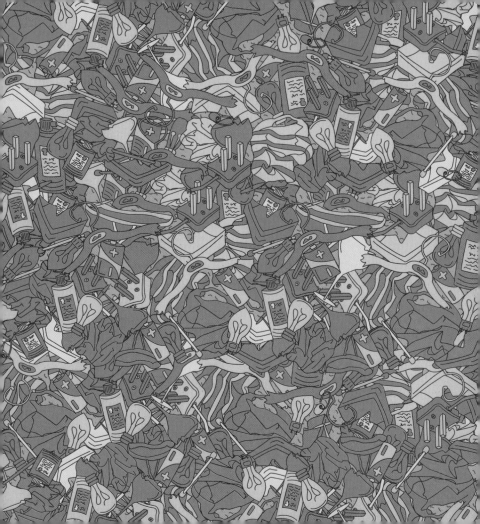

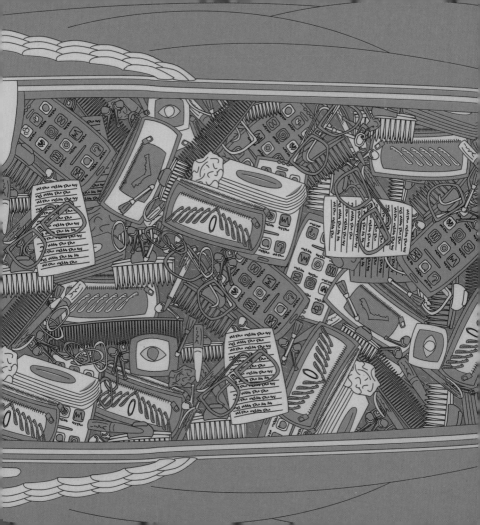

SEARCH YOUR BATHROOM CABINET

FIND THEM IN THE FLOWER BED

FIND THEM IN THE FRUIT BOWL

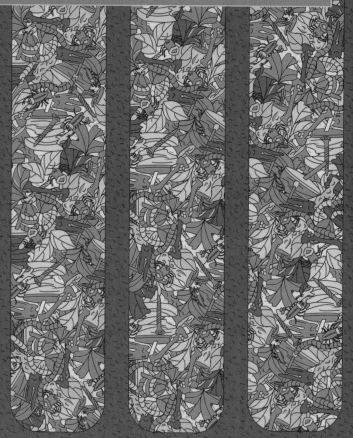
YOU DROPPED THEM DOWN A DRAIN!

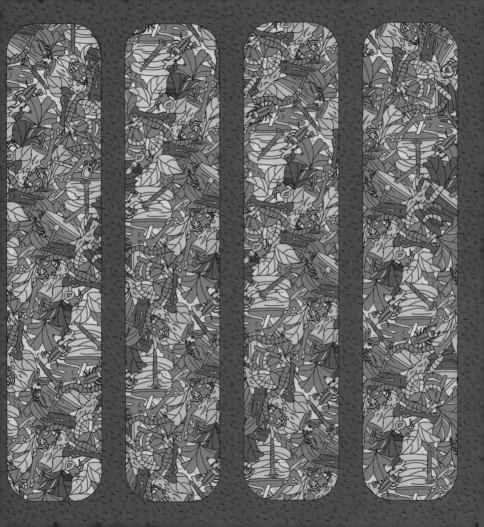

ARE THEY IN YOUR JEWELLERY BOX?

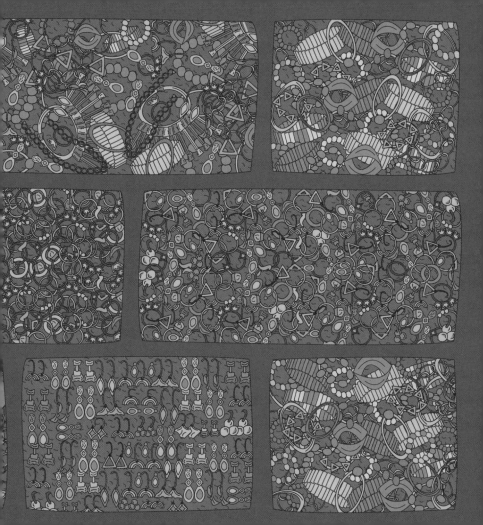

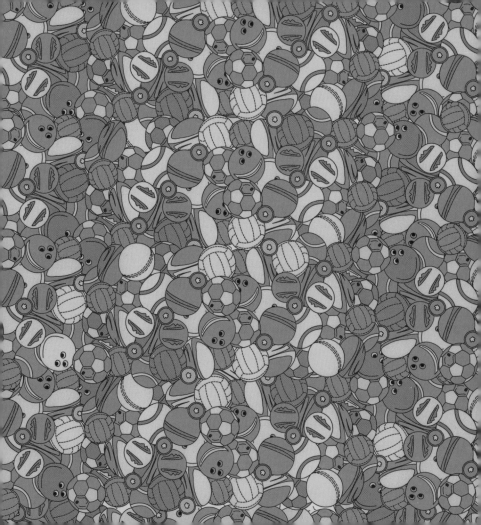

GET YOUR HANDS WET!

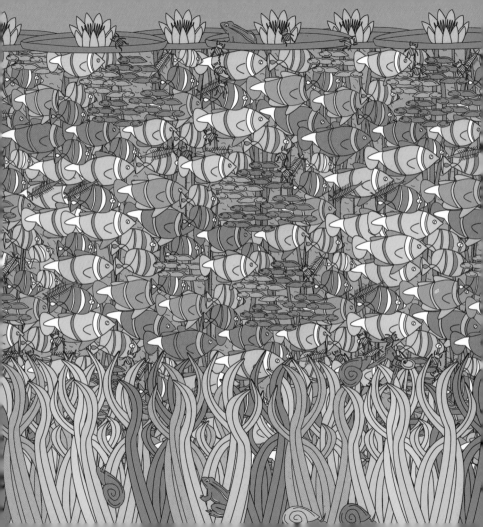

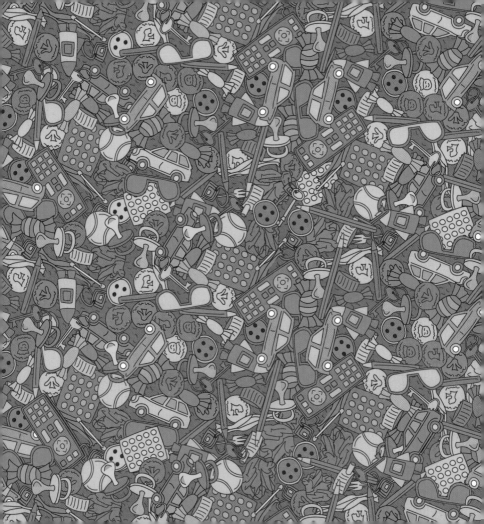

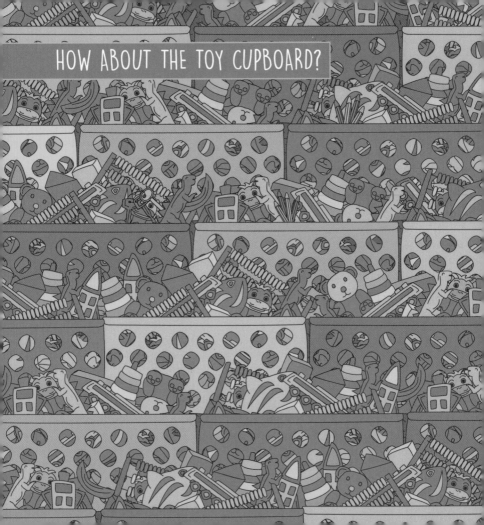

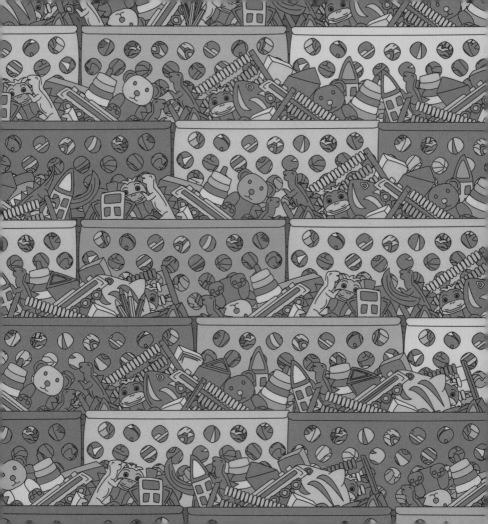

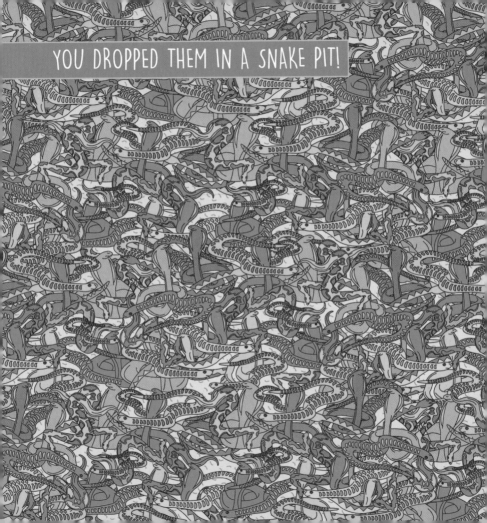

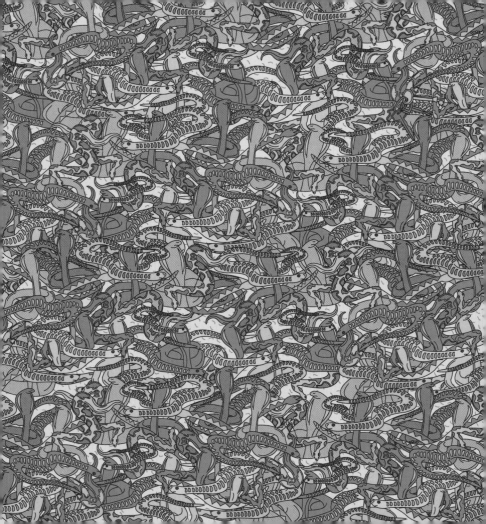

OR AT THE BOOKSHOP?

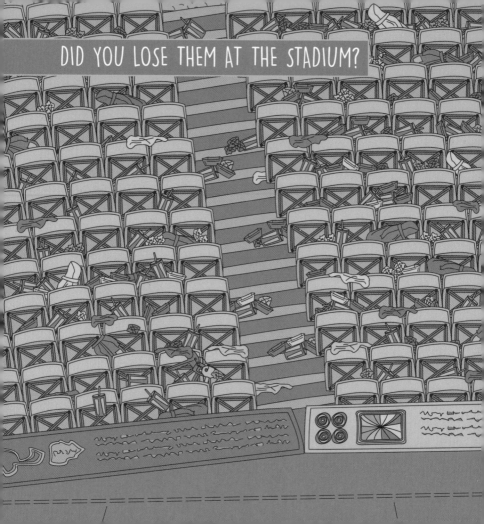

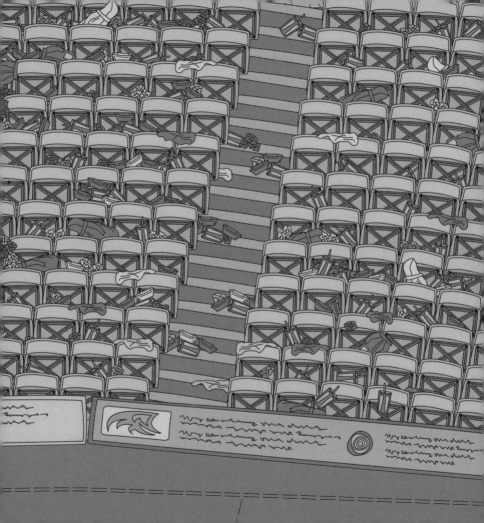

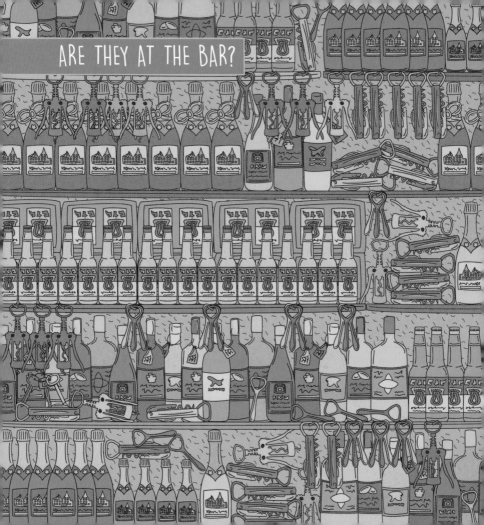

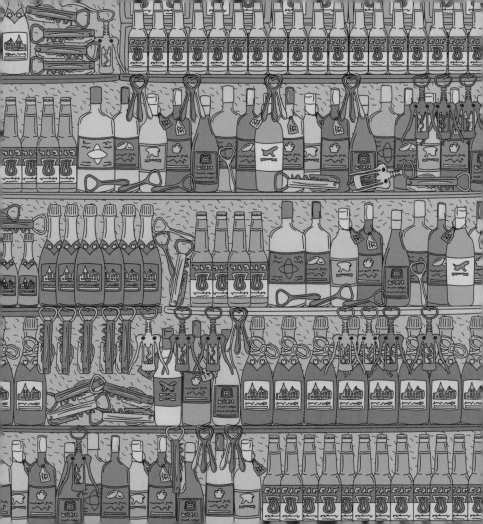

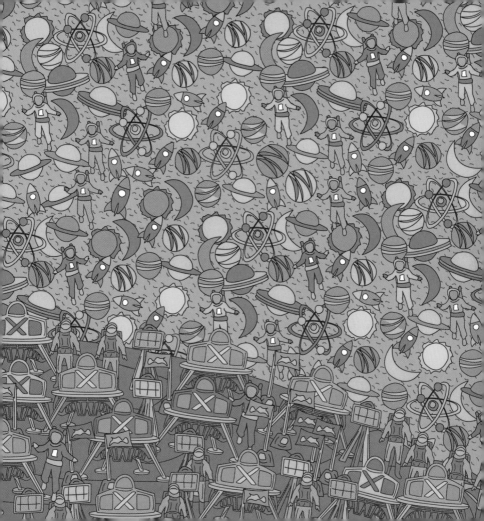

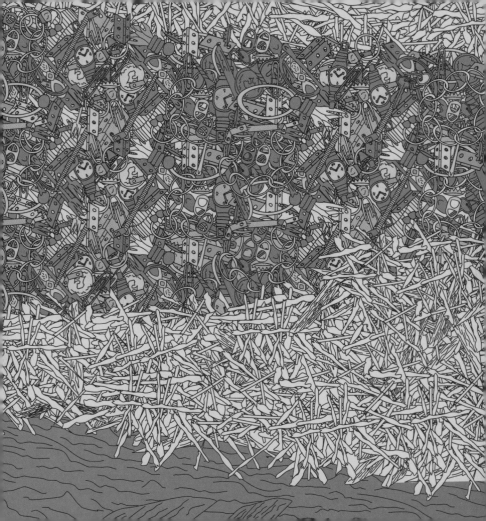

TRY SOME MEDITATION...

DID YOU LOSE THEM CAMPING?

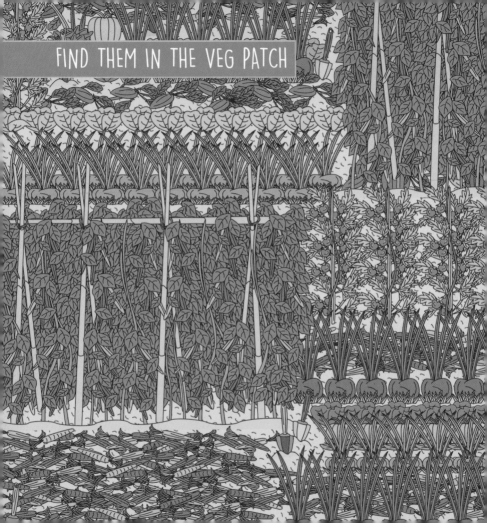

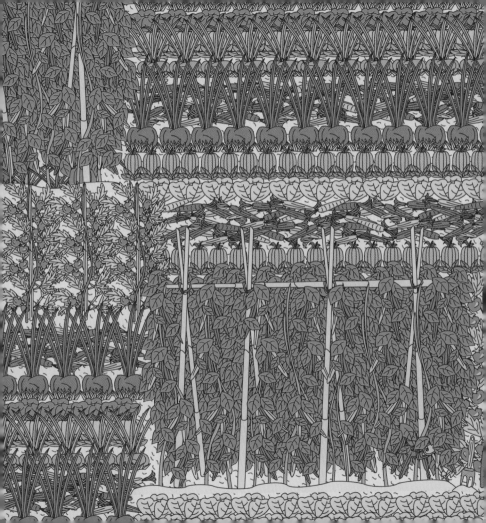

TRY THE SHOE SHOP

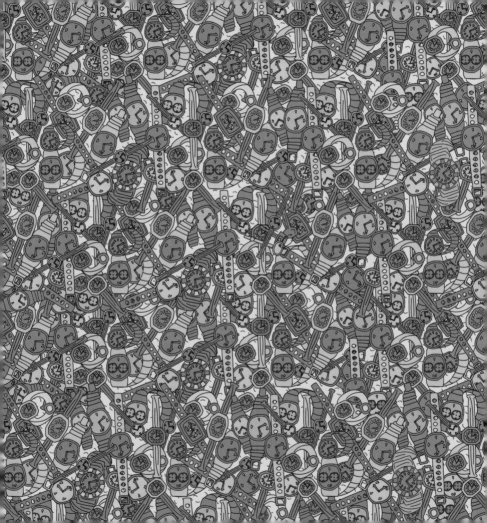

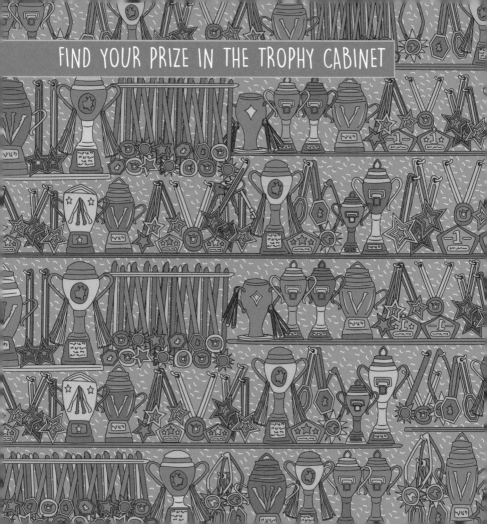

FIND YOUR PRIZE IN THE TROPHY CABINET

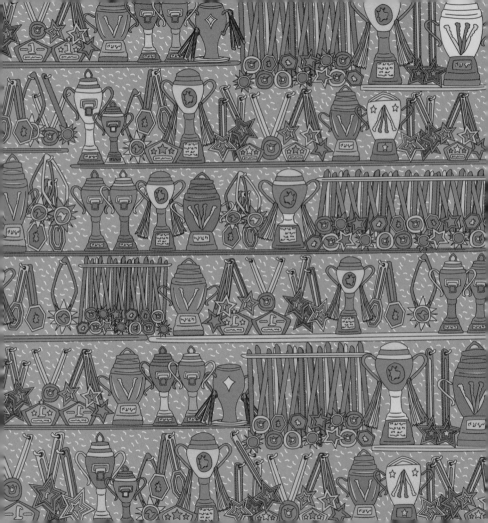

ARE THEY HAUNTING THE HALLOWEEN PARTY?

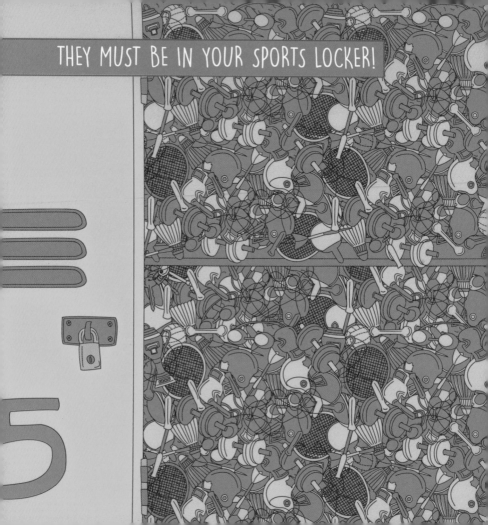

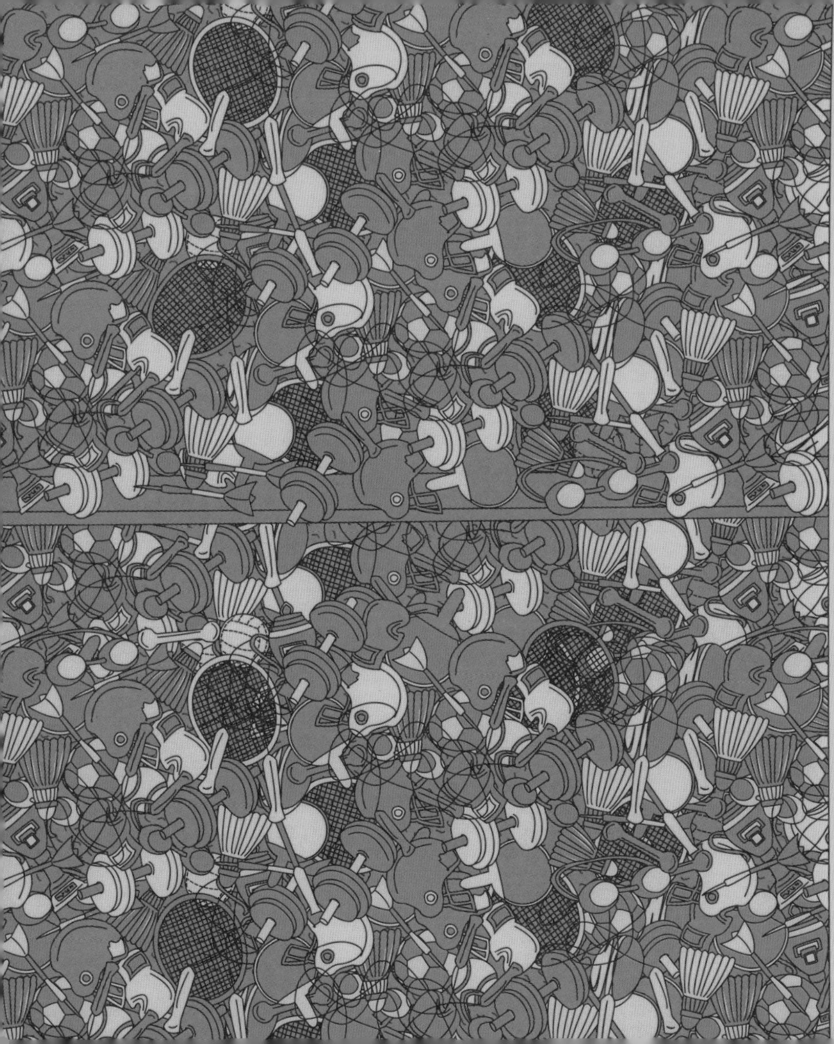

FIND THEM IN THE CUTLERY DRAWER

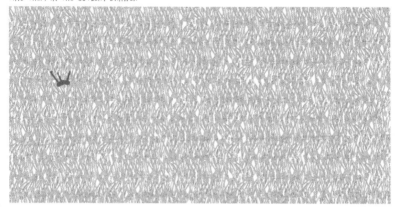

DID YOU DROP THEM IN THE SOCK PILE?

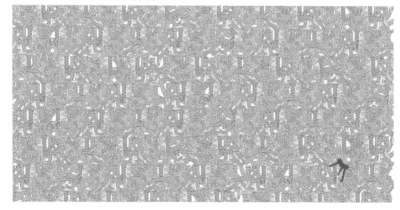

RUMMAGE AMONG THE POTTED PLANTS

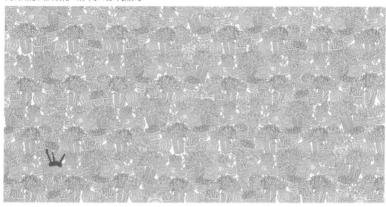

ARE THEY IN YOUR TOOL BOX?

GET IN WITH THE CREEPY-CRAWLIES

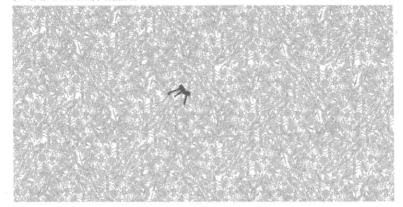

YOU DROPPED THEM IN THE WASTE BASKET!

FIND THEM IN THE BATTERIES BOX

SEARCH AMONG THE BULBS

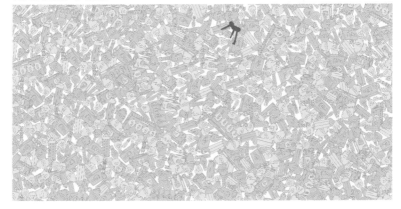

DID YOU DROP THEM IN THE FOOD WASTE?

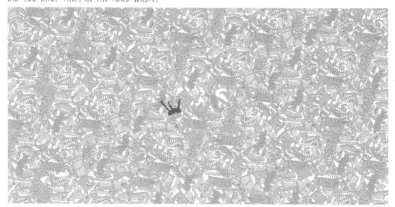

ARE THEY IN YOUR HANDBAG?

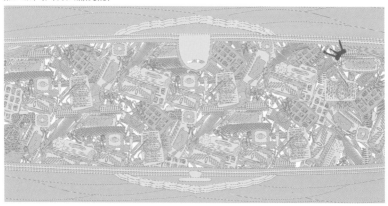

SEARCH YOUR BATHROOM CABINET

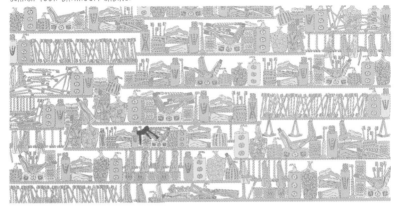

FIND THEM IN THE FLOWER BED

ARE THEY IN THE CLEANING CUPBOARD?

HAVE A LOOK IN THE LAUNDRY BASKET

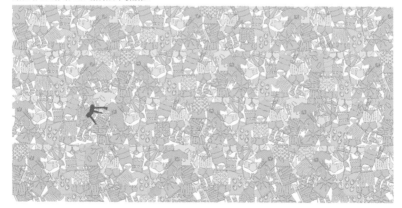

FIND THEM IN THE FRUIT BOWL

YOU DROPPED THEM DOWN A DRAIN!

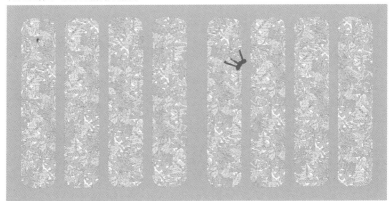

DID YOU LEAVE THEM IN THE GARDEN SHED?

HOW ABOUT THE COFFEE SHOP?

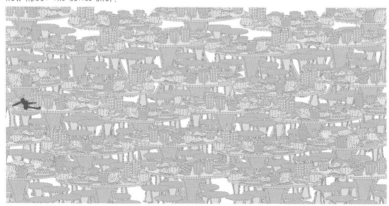

ARE THEY IN YOUR JEWELLERY BOX?

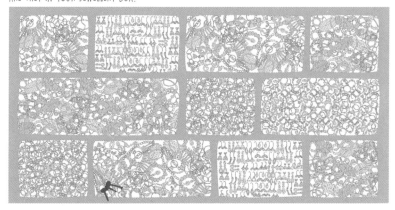

DID YOU DROP THEM ON THE BEACH?

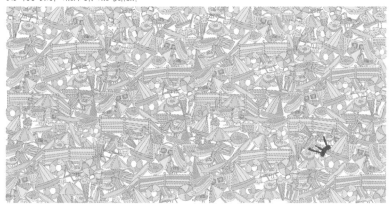

THEY MUST BE IN THE BALL PIT!

GET YOUR HANDS WET!

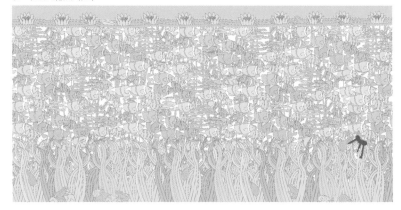

DID YOU LEAVE THEM AT THE OFFICE?

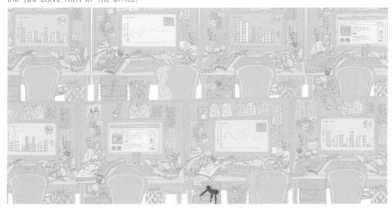

DOWN THE BACK OF THE SOFA?

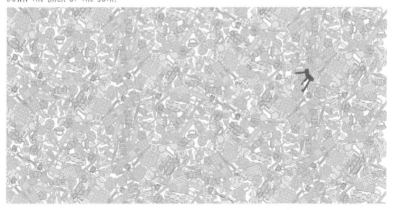

HOW ABOUT THE TOY CUPBOARD?

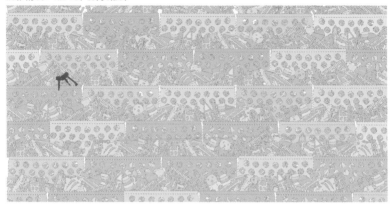

YOU DROPPED THEM IN A SNAKE PIT!

ARE THEY AT THE GOLF CLUB?

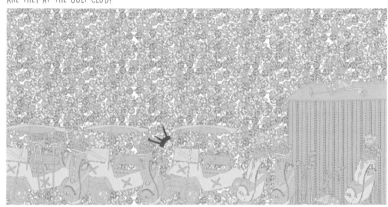

OR AT THE BOOKSHOP?

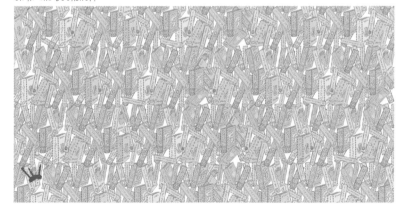

DID YOU LOSE THEM AT THE STADIUM?

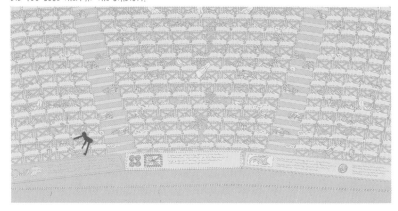

ARE THEY AT THE BAR?

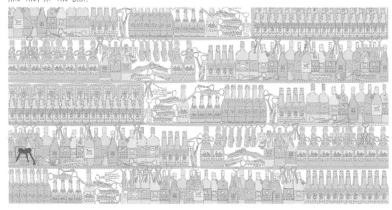

THEY MUST BE IN OUTER SPACE!

YOU DROPPED THEM ON THE PISTE!

THE MAGPIE MUST HAVE TAKEN THEM!

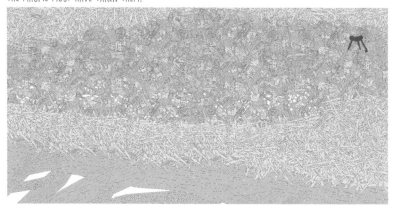

TRY SOME MEDITATION...

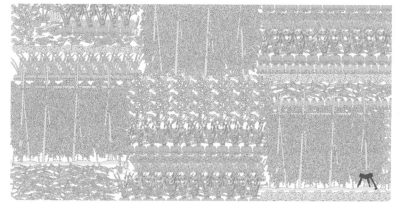

TRY THE SHOE SHOP

RUMMAGE AMONG THE WATCHES

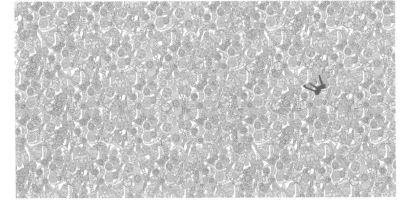

FIND YOUR PRIZE IN THE TROPHY CABINET

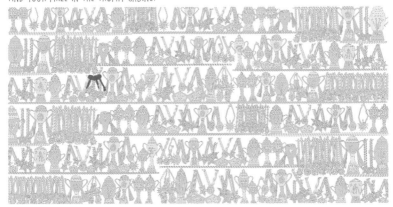

YOU DROPPED THEM IN THE CAR PARK!

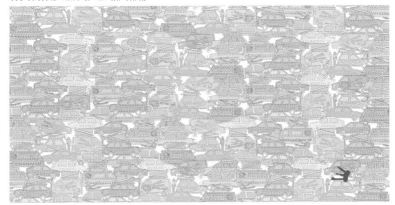

ARE THEY HAUNTING THE HALLOWEEN PARTY?

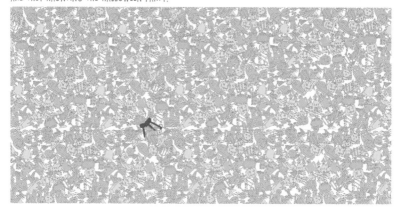

THEY MUST BE IN YOUR SPORTS LOCKER!